BASIC ASTROLOGY

for the

SCORPIO KID

October 24th - November 21st

BASIC ASTROLOGY

for the

SCORPIO KID

October 24th - November 21st

Barry D. McCollough
and Yvonne Sullivan

Dedicated to our benevolent ancestors,
known and unknown,
and to our future generations.

ISBN: 979-8-53060-039-5 (Paperback)

Dear Reader:

Welcome to the "Basic Astrology for Kids" series. Are you ready to go on a journey to discover more about Western astrology and your zodiac sign? My goal is to help you develop an appreciation for astrology. Also, I hope to spark within you an interest in biology, chemistry, meteorology and the sciences through your interest in astrology.

Growing up in my family, we found astrology to be a "gateway" to our study of both science and the classics in school. I hope that you will also be so inspired.

In studying astrology, you will journey back to a time when hunter, gatherer and farmer families shared stories around the campfire. These were stories of Gods, Goddesses, and talking animals who were a "real" part of their belief system. We hope these shared memories will also inspire you, as a young reader, to reverence our great ancestors who lay the foundations for our lives.

Barry D. McCollough
Master Astrologer

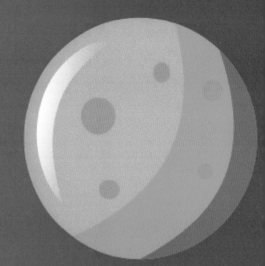

Astrology is an ancient system of belief that grew out of our ancestors' natural curiosity about stars twinkling in the night sky. There are many systems of astrology, including Tropical, Vedic, Sidereal, and Chinese. Tropical astrology, also known as Western, is the focus of this book.

In Western astrology, zodiac signs relate to specific star patterns (or constellations) that occur regularly at certain times and places in the night sky. There are a total of 12 zodiac signs. Each sign occupies a 30 degree portion of the 360 degree orbit around the Sun.

You are a Scorpio because you were born between Ocotober 24th and November 21st. The symbol for Scorpio is the scorpion. You like to explore mysteries.

As the sun passes through the zodiac signs in the course of a year, the seasons change. There are four seasons:

WINTER

SPRING

AUTUMN

SUMMER

As a Scorpio, you were born during the Autumn season. Chilly nights call for warm sweaters. Leaves on the trees turn brown, yellow, and orange.

You share the Autumn season with . . .

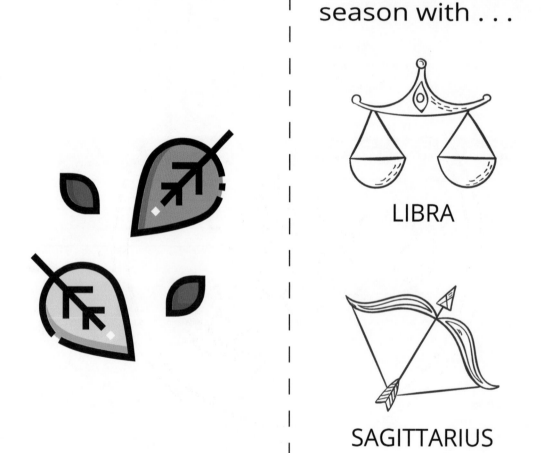

LIBRA

SAGITTARIUS

Star patterns, or constellations, are shapes of humans, animals, and other things that our ancestors imagined as they gazed at the stars in the night sky.

The Scorpion is the star pattern of Scorpio. Tiny, yet powerful, the lightning-quick barb at the tip of his tail is the great equalizer.

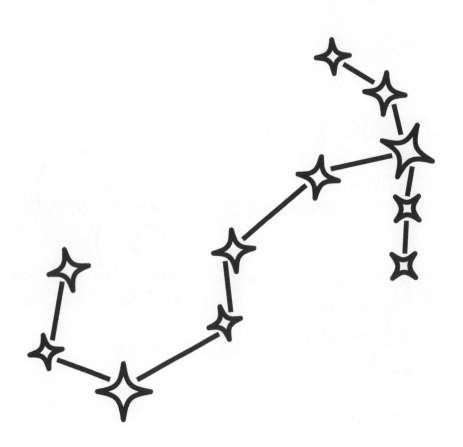

In Western astrology, houses are not physical places but are fields of experience that each zodiac sign passes through in the course of a year. There are 12 houses, each with unique characteristics:

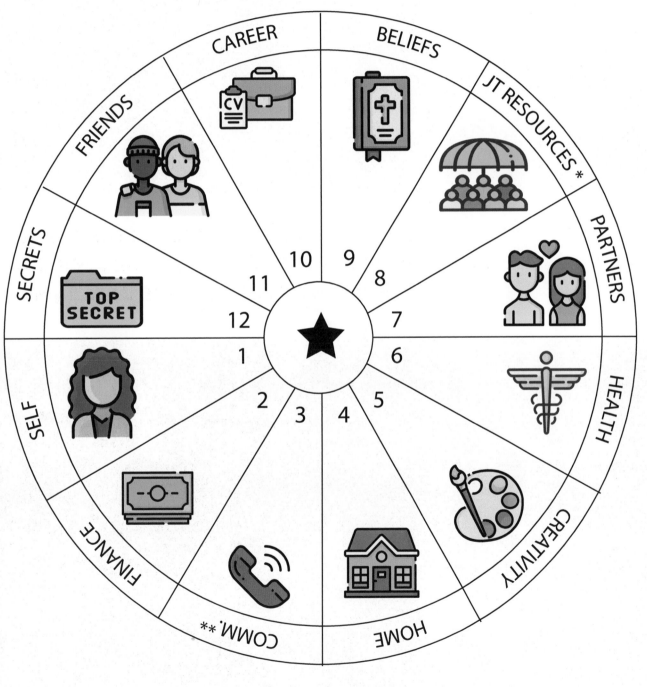

*JOINT RESOURCES
**COMMUNICATION

As a Scorpio, the 8th House keeps you forever connected to matters related to taxes, insurance, inheritance, and shared resources.

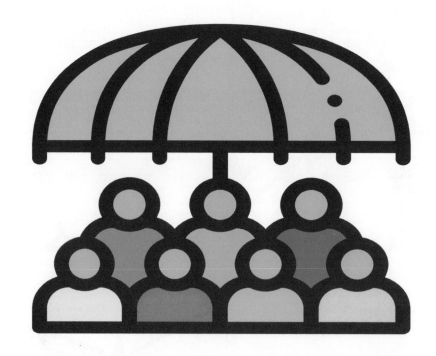

8TH HOUSE - JOINT RESEOURCES

In Western astrology, polarity defines opposites among the zodiac signs. A zodiac sign will have either an active or receptive polarity. Active polarity is more assertive and expressive. Receptive polarity is more passive and reactive. The Yin Yang symbol below is an example of polarity.

Born a Scorpio, your polarity is receptive. You can be emotional. Taurus is your calm opposite.

In Western astrology, modality determines how a person approaches life. The 12 zodiac signs are divided into 3 types of modalities:

| CARDINAL | FIXED | MUTABLE |
DYNAMIC	DETERMINED	ADAPTABLE
ARIES	TAURUS	GEMINI
CANCER	LEO	VIRGO
LIBRA	SCORPIO	SAGITTARIUS
CAPRICORN	AQUARIUS	PISCES

Born a Scorpio, your modality is fixed. You are reliable, stubborn, and love to be secure.

FIXED

In Western astrology, the 12 zodiac signs are divided into 4 groups of natural elements: fire, earth, air, and water. These elements help a person understand their personality and how they relate to others and to nature.

FIRE

AIR

EARTH

WATER

Born a Scorpio, your natural element is water. You like to investigate and solve mysteries.

You share the water element with . . .

CANCER

PISCES

Each zodiac sign is represented by a color that highlights its best known traits.

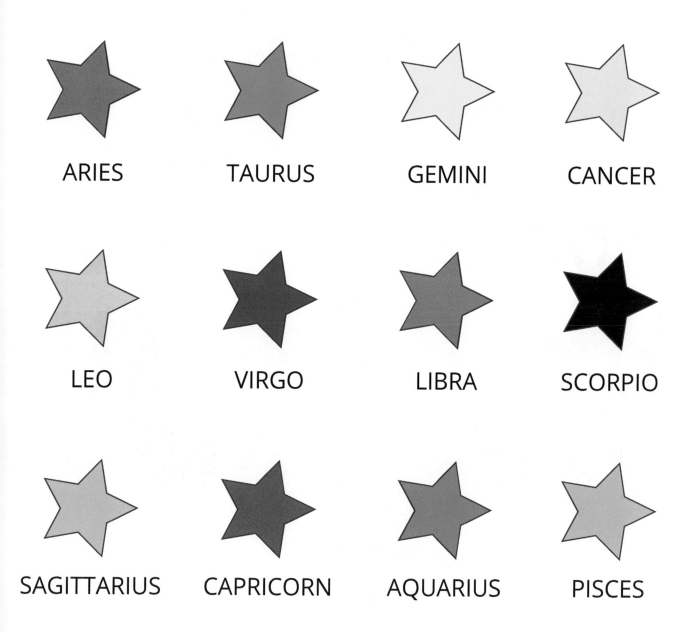

ARIES

TAURUS

GEMINI

CANCER

LEO

VIRGO

LIBRA

SCORPIO

SAGITTARIUS

CAPRICORN

AQUARIUS

PISCES

In Western astrology, each zodiac sign has a ruling planet, except for Cancer and Leo. Cancer is ruled by the Moon, which is considered a "natural satellite." Leo is ruled by the Sun, which is considered a star. Ruling planets have been observed for thousands of years by our ancestors and express the characteristics of the zodiac signs. Some of the ruling planets are considered to be mythical gods and goddesses.

Pluto is the ruling planet of Scorpio. Pluto is the God of the Underworld. Ruled by Pluto, you are a natural investigator and are very secretive.

GLYPHS

Glyphs are simple characters that represent the zodiac signs and other astrological concepts. Check them out below:

ZODIAC

♈	♉	♊	♋
ARIES	TAURUS	GEMINI	CANCER
♌	♍	♎	♏
LEO	VIRGO	LIBRA	SCORPIO
♐	♑	♒	♓
SAGITTARIUS	CAPRICORN	AQUARIUS	PISCES

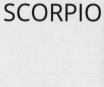

GLOSSARY

ELEMENTS

WATER

EARTH

AIR

FIRE

RULING PLANETS

MARS

VENUS

MERCURY

MODALITY

CARDINAL

MOON

SUN

PLUTO

FIXED

JUPITER

URANUS

NEPTUNE

MUTABLE

Putting it all together for you, Scorpio!

SCORPIO
ZODIAC
SYMBOL

WATER
ELEMENT
SYMBOL

FIXED
MODALITY
GLYPH

RECEPTIVE
POLARITY

SCORPIO
ZODIAC
GLYPH

WATER
ELEMENT
GLYPH

BORN IN
AUTUMN

TAURUS
POLARITY
OPPOSITE

8TH HOUSE
JOINT
RESOURCES

PLUTO
RULING
PLANET

THE SCORPION
STAR PATTERN

PLUTO
RULING
PLANET
GLYPH

PLUTO
"GOD OF THE
UNDERWORLD"

BEST
COLOR

Barry D. McCollough - Master Astrologer & Co-Author

My parents had a backyard garden when I was growing up. They grew a host of vegetables served at the dinner table. I remember they introduced me to the farmer's almanac they consulted to grow their crops. I was fascinated by the book. My attention was drawn to a host of strange symbols that populated some of the pages. I learned that these strange symbols tracked the passage of the Moon through the signs of the zodiac.

Shortly after I started reading about Moon signs in the almanac, I started calculating astrological charts for myself and family members. By the time I graduated from high school, I was doing astrological forecasts for many people. As of 2021, I have been practicing astrological divination since 1970 or for 51 years. I earned a B.A. in English and American Literature from Brown University and a M.A. in Communication from Stanford University.

As I contemplate passing my gardening habits to my granddaughter, there are two things I feel are important. First, I hope my astrological study and years of practice are shared with future generations through my writing. And second, I must continue to reinforce family traditions so that my future generations are blessed to partake of garden fresh vegetables at their dinner tables.

www.barrydmccollough.com

Yvonne Sullivan - Numerologist & Co-Author

I am a numerologist and licensed CPA. Many of the women in my family have special gifts. My special gift is being able to help others get answers to their questions about life. I call myself the Queen of NOC.

I have studied numerology for over 20 years. The subject considers how numbers and letters have secret meanings. My attraction to numerology is unsurprising because I love numbers. Math was one of my favorite subjects in school. My college degree is a B.B.A. in Accounting.

I talk with my angels so I can help others. The way we talk is unique. We have a special language. It includes numbers and symbols. I also get messages from my angels in my dreams.

I enjoy reading and writing when I have free time.

www.yvonnesullivan.com

Thank you for reading this book. Please take a few minutes to leave a positive review online wherever the "Basic Astrology for Kids" series is sold.

All 12 books in the "Basic Astrology for Kids" series:

  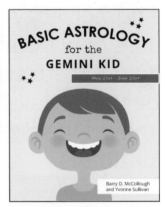 

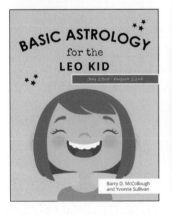  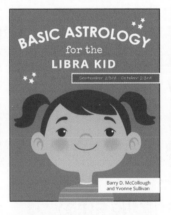 

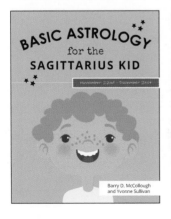  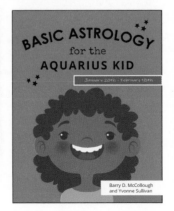 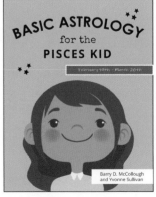

Printed in Great Britain
by Amazon

13697623R00020